# TINTAGEL REFLECTIONS

BOSSINEY BOOKS

1

Published in 1994 by Bossiney Books, St Teath, Bodmin, Cornwall.

Typeset and printed by Penwell Ltd, Callington, Cornwall

ISBN 0 948158 89 1

**ACKNOWLEDGEMENTS**
Front cover: ROY WESTLAKE
Front cover design: MAGGIE GINGER
Modern photographs: RAY BISHOP
Drawings: FELICITY YOUNG

*Authors' Acknowledgements*
We are indebted once more to the photography of Ray Bishop and to Roy Westlake
for his evocative cover shot. Our thanks to Sally Dodd for typing the manuscript
and Angela Larcombe for her editing.

*Books Consulted:*
**The Parish of Tintagel**, Canon AC Canner; **King Arthur in the West**, Felicity
Young and Michael Williams; **Tintagel**, Michael Williams.

# About the Authors

*MICHAEL WILLIAMS, a Cornishman, started full-time publishing in 1975. He and his wife Sonia live in a cottage on the shoulder of a green valley just outside St Teath in North Cornwall. Before that they lived for ten years at Bossiney; in that time Michael's interest in the subject of Arthur deepened and broadened.*

*He has broadcast and written extensively on Arthur and related subjects, his earlier works include a guide to Tintagel, still in print, and he is co-author of* King Arthur Country.

*A member of the Ghost Club, his recent publications include* Supernatural Investigation *and* Psychic Phenomena of the West. *A member of the International League for the Protection of Horses and the RSPCA he has, over the years, worked hard for reform in laws relating to animal welfare.*

*FELICITY YOUNG lives at Tintagel with her husband Ian, daughter Hazel, horse Red and dog Digger. She is a painter, book illustrator and author. Since 1984 she has contributed more than 350 illustrations for a whole range of Bossiney titles – a number of her drawings appear inside these pages.*

*Felicity Young is the co-author of* King Arthur in the West, *and in 1993 she made two radio broadcasts on Arthur and his links with the Westcountry. She did an earlier broadcast on the craft of illustrating books.*

*In 1989 she made her debut as a Bossiney author, contributing a chapter on Lawrence of Arabia in* Dorset Mysteries. *Then in 1990 came her first book* Curiosities of Exmoor. *In 1991 she wrote about Charlotte Bryant, a small-time prostitute in* Strange Dorset Stories *and the following year she explored 'Strange Places', a chapter in* Strange Stories of Cornwall.

*Michael Williams*

*Felicity Young*

# Tintagel Reflections

TINTAGEL is a magical area of Cornwall. The magic is in the beauty of the coastline – and in the way it fires our imagination.

You cannot 'do' Tintagel in an afternoon or a day. Tintagel is an ongoing experience. I knew a man who had first come to Tintagel in 1919. He kept coming back, rediscovering the place until his death some sixty years later.

Arthur Mee, the travel writer, came to this corner of North Cornwall in the 1930s researching his book *Cornwall,* and this is how he responded:

*'It is an incomparable piece of this incomparable coast. Its rocks rise sheer from the sea, crowned with green carpets, with fragments of ancient walls creeping over them, with lichen-covered caps and moss-grown ways and tiny caves, and what is left of an old monk's chapel, here a doorway, here a window, here a graveyard, with one of Cornwall's oldest churches looking down on the waters of the Atlantic sweeping in below.'*

Of course, if Mr Mee came back tomorrow, he would see great changes – and not all of them for the better, but where development has not sprawled, Tintagel remains a worthwhile North Cornwall experience.

The visitor who points his camera in the direction of Tintagel Castle, and hurries away, sees next to nothing. Edmund Sedding, my old tutor, taught me 'history' comes from a Greek word meaning 'investigation'. I have often thought of Edmund on my journeys around Tintagel; this place is worthy of investigation or, at very least, a spirit of curiosity. Tintagel, like good claret, should be enjoyed slowly, and remember, if you can avoid the height of the holiday season, then the odds are you will enjoy it most. Remember too, we have some beautiful diamond sharp days in the winter.

For generations Tintagel has inspired creativity. Writers and painters have attempted to pin the quality and qualities to paper and on to canvas. Tennyson and Swinburne both wrote major poems in its honour. The last movement of Elgar's Second Symphony was written here, Sir Arnold Bax's tone poem 'Tintagel' has given pleasure to music lovers in many countries. In 1818 J M W Turner, the greatest of English painters, painted the Castle: too fanciful for some people maybe but immensely powerful in terms of drama and atmosphere.

Tintagel Castle

*Artist Felicity Young captures the magic and mystery of Tintagel Castle.*

Arthur, of course, is a powerful magnet. Though the historian may say Tintagel Castle was built centuries after Arthur lived and fought the English, there is little doubt there was a King Arthur here in the west, and Tintagel is the garden of many Arthurian tales and his Court of Camelot. From the medieval romances through to T H White and Mary Stewart in this century, Arthur has triggered more story-telling than any other legendary figure.

A travel writer earlier in this century gives us this sharp word portrait of the village.

*'Tintagel, to those who knew it some years ago, presents a curious mixture of the old and the new. It has not altered its familiar features; the shapes of the street, the grey slate cottages, the low quaint dwellings, are still there; but they are incongruously mixed with modern erections. Tintagel is Trevena grown up. The change of name is a remarkable example of the influence of the visitor upon Cornwall. Years ago this*

7

*A chunk of cliffscape, photographed by Ray Bishop in the late 1970s.*

post town was Trevena; and letters had to be so addressed. Tintagel only applied to the headland "Dundagel", where King Arthur's Castle stands, and to the parish. In course of time the whole place became known as Tintagel by reason of a post office decision to that effect, and, though the name of Trevena is still correctly used of the village, Tintagel, the place is to the outside world.'

As a member of the Ghost Club and someone who has been investigating the supernatural for more than a quarter of a century, I have been impressed by the high percentage of hauntings in the Tintagel district. Why this should be the case continues to mystify. Time itself is something of a mystery and in my supernatural investigations I have often had the impression that time can run backwards. The term 'time slip' in the supernatural field means occasions when people somehow find themselves in the past, and this sort of experience has occurred with surprising frequency in this part of North Cornwall. Ghostly monks, fleeting glimpses of King Arthur himself, paranormal music, invisible footsteps: these are only some of the claims which make Tintagel one of the most haunted regions in the whole of the Westcountry.

The other side of the coin – or is it a different shade of the same side? – is that many religious people find a deeply spiritual atmosphere hereabouts. The local churches are living testimony of the saints who brought the Christian message all those years ago, while the chapels are legacies of John Wesley and his fiery message.

On the cliffs and inland at the remoter spots, one occasionally feels in touch with a distant past. Dame Daphne du Maurier once told me in certain parts of ancient Kernow she felt 'like an astronaut in time'. I know precisely what she meant – and have felt it strongly in or near Tintagel, especially out of the holiday season.

Then the present disappears and past years vanish, making a mockery of history and the thing we call time.

# Tintagel

TO STAND on these cliffs at Tintagel is a great edge of the ocean experience. They have a certain defiance. A painter or a writer can be tempted to over-romanticise North Cornwall or parts of her, but at Tintagel you see beauty mingling with the cruel and the wicked as sea and land are locked in their eternal struggle.

Invariably I come away from them refreshed and renewed. In that mood Tintagel is a worthwhile experience – and often a new beginning.

For many overseas visitors Tintagel is a kind of pilgrimage. The very word fires their imagination. It would be a very dull man or woman who came and stood here, particularly on the headland, and did not feel a sense of awe and wonder.

Tintagel's ability to cast its spell was well demonstrated in the life and times of Frederick Thomas Glasscock, a millionaire, a partner in the famous custard firm of Monkhouse and Glasscock, he came to Cornwall to retire but instead, falling in love with the Arthurian romances and seeing their commercial possibilities, founded the Fellowship of the Order of the Round Table, and started reaping a second fortune. He died in 1934, aboard the *Queen Mary*, on his way to the United States and was buried at sea.

He would have been proud to see the revival of his Fellowship of the Knights of the Round Table of King Arthur in 1993, the Diamond Jubilee of these magnificent halls.

9

*The knighting of Sir Galahad by Sir Lancelot – one of a number of fine Arthurian paintings by William Hatherell RI, on show at King Arthur's Great Halls. These oil paintings, in a highly attractive figurative style, were especially commissioned and are all taken from descriptions in Malory's Morte d'Arthur. They remind us how the tales of Arthur have inspired a good deal of creativity over the years.*

*'Non-sectarian, non-political, non-denominational without creed or bias and truly international, the Fellowship aims to bring together men and women from all corners of the earth, where a sense of belonging and communication can bring pleasure, knowledge and contact that will enrich the lives of everyone.'*

Mr Glasscock may be gone, but King Arthur's Great Halls in the main street of the village are his superb legacies. They are open to the public and remain an essential destination on any real Arthurian tour of the west.

Times were when this coastline was the haunt of smugglers. For a matter of two hundred years there was 'war' between our North Cornwall smugglers and the Revenue. Writers, particularly those of fiction, tend to portray those smugglers as rich young men with an appetite for adventure rather than law breaking, and occasionally as double agents in the struggles between these islands and France, but in reality they were very different: the perpetrators of deeds stained with murder, treachery and violence.

Traditional smuggling followed fishing and mining as the great Cornish industries, and all layers of society participated: the gentry bought their wines and lace at 'cut' prices; now and then Customs House men connived, and there were whispered allegations about magistrates and ministers of the church.

Parson Hawker of Morwenstow has given us a fine word picture of the smuggling operation:

*'The rough sea-captain, half smuggler, half pirate, who ran his lugger by beacon-light into some rugged cove among the massive headlands of the shore, and was relieved of his freight by the active and diligent "countryside". This was the term allotted to that chosen troop of native sympathisers who were always ready to rescue and conceal the stories that had escaped the degradation of the gauger's brand. Men yet alive relate with glee how they used to rush at some well-known signal to the strand, their small active horses shaved from forelock to tail, smoother than any modern clip, well soaped or greased from head to foot, so as to slip easily out of any hostile grasp; and then with a double keg or pack slung on to every nag by a single girth, away went the whole herd led by some swift well trained mare, to the inland cave or rocky hold, the shelter of their spoil.'*

This corner of North Cornwall is rich too in legend. There are the leg-

11

ends of St Nectan and his beautiful glen, remarkable tales about Sir Francis Drake who, though a Devon man, was a member of Parliament for Bossiney, the bells of Forrabury Church at Boscastle, and Cruel Coppinger, savage leader of a gang of wreckers.

Not for nothing has Cornwall been called the Land of Legend – sometimes also the Land of Merlin. Myth, of course, down the ages has triggered all the great story-telling. As for folklore, I seriously doubt whether there is such a thing as pure legend, no grain of truth. Our Cornish legends resemble the old game of 'Chinese Whispers.' First comes the original tale, and then, with the passing of time, the tales continue to rumble on – subtle additions and sometimes distortion.

Cruel Coppinger, the evil wrecker, is a good example. Is it completely safe to assume he never lived? There are documented facts indicating that a Coppinger really was around the North Cornwall-North Devon coasts. But the key question is 'Which Coppinger?'

Here we ought to consider the question of Arthur. Does he belong to reality or legend?

As a result of serious research, more and more people believe Arthur was a probability rather than a possibility, and a percentage is convinced there was *an* Arthur.

Arthur's victories were achieved at a time when written records were scarce, and his reputation spread through word of mouth, and we can guess each achievement grew in the telling and retelling.

When I first came to Bossiney in 1965 I rated Arthur a spectacular personality belonging to legend, but after more than a quarter of a century of reading, researching, and listening to experts on the subject, my view has changed.

Arthur almost certainly did live and operate here in the Westcountry, but not as a king who neatly fits the monarch presiding over the glamorous Court of Camelot, a setting and image created in the fertile imaginations of authors, poets and painters.

I have interviewed members of a psycho-expansion group here in the South West, men and women holding responsible worthwhile jobs today. They claim to have lived in earlier lives in the days of King Arthur – some even claim they were Arthurian characters and several members of that group say Arthur was here in Cornwall, but that he had a roving command which accounts for his presence in other places, notably Somerset.

*Smugglers land their cargo on a Tintagel beach.*

Psycho-expansion, of course, not only goes back to earlier lives and times. The other side and claim of the psycho-expansion coin is that it is able to travel forward in the thing we call time. In one interview with a character who claimed to have been Arthur himself came this prediction: one day the reality of Arthur will be proved – and proved here in North Cornwall.

Outside and beyond all this, the mystery deepens in that there is no certain known Arthur grave. By burying his bones in an unmarked grave, his commanders saved them from future desecration. So, in an odd fashion, Arthur's fame grew in death. So much so that some believed he had not died, and would, one day, reappear to drive out the foes of Britain.

It is up to us, as individuals, to make up our own minds about the character of Arthur.

But nobody can deny that personalities like Arthur and Guinevere, Merlin and Lancelot are deeply rooted in British tradition and culture.

In British story-telling Arthur lives on, and perhaps more significantly in hearts and minds, all of which leads us naturally to the Grail Tradition. This is the embodiment of a dream, and though the legends of the Holy Grail are wrapped in mystery, we soon discover Arthur is essentially about a search – our search – and at the very heart of the matter is an effort to discover our best self – or selves.

\*　　\*　　\*　　\*　　\*

*And as Michael Williams ends his reflections on Tintagel, Felicity Young begins to paint her own portrait of the Cornish village that means so much to her.*

*A postcard from the thirties, showing the remains of the mill.*

# King Arthur's Castle

THE TRACK leading down to the Castle ruins is very uneven and steep. In the summer it is swarming with visitors who readily stop and buy ice cream from a cleverly positioned van. This road descends what is now called the Vale of Avalon, the approach to King Arthur's Castle. Part of the way down is a little stone bridge and the remains of a building. It is hard to imagine that this pile of fallen stones was once a working mill, the Old Borough Mill. It was described by the traveller William Howitt in 1867 as a *'picturesque old mill stuck in a nook … whose large over-shot wheel sent the water splashing and splattering down into a rocky basin beneath …'*

The postcard dated September 6 1934 reminds us of the mill's past existence by the ruined wall standing out clearly in the valley. There is a somewhat newer cottage on the same site, the home of a famous Tintagel character, Florence Nightingale Richards, it too is now nothing more than a ruin. Florence was the keeper of the keys to Tintagel Castle for many years and continued to escort parties of visitors around the island well into her old age; she delighted all with her stories, pointing out King Arthur's footstep, a dent in the rock where he was supposed to have placed one foot on the island and one on the church tower. She was a short dark woman of rugged appearance who could have stepped straight out of the Arthurian Legends.

# Castle Cove

BELOW the ruins of Tintagel Castle is a little cove, a natural harbour in which to shelter from the ravages of the Atlantic Ocean. It is no longer used for the landing of goods as it once was, each year the access to the beach becomes more and more difficult. Rockfalls are commonplace and the Castle 'Island' is gradually becoming just that as the narrow isthmus is slowly eroded away. A postcard sent from Tintagel to a lady in Plymouth was postmarked September 1910, some years before a major landslide in 1918 virtually cut off the island. Now the only way across is by a concrete bridge and many exhausting steps.

Each year the island has to be closed while vital work is carried out on the rockface to ensure the safety of the thousands of visitors who come to explore Tintagel Castle. The steps going down to the beach are slippery and quite treacherous at times. Once on the beach, surrounded by the towering cliffs which echo with the cries of gulls nesting in the rocky crags, the sense of history is overwhelming. You can almost hear the clamour of the men working to load up their little boats with slate, their shouts reverberating around the rocks, blending with the calls of the seabirds.

Looking at this postcard it seems hard to imagine this cove as a bustling port, but many old photographs show ships beached, awaiting their cargo of slate from the nearby quarries. A gantry can be seen on the left of the picture, it was used with a system of pulleys to load the slate onto the boats. It could be a risky business as the sea was unpredictable and from time to time a small boat would be smashed to pieces on the rocks by an unusually large swell.

Merlin's Cave adds a touch of mystery to the cove. It extends right through the rocks beneath the Castle Island. Dark and awesome, legend says this is where Merlin discovered the infant Arthur, directly below the ruins of Tintagel Castle. Pictures taken around 1880 show a narrow

Tintagel.

wooden bridge crossing in front of the mouth of the cave. It was at this time a shaft was sunk beyond Merlin's cave to mine for silver-lead, the bridge being the access for the workers. Unfortunately there was insufficient ore to make the mine viable and it failed. Slate continued to be shipped from the cove but as we can see from the postcard of 1910 the wooden bridge across the cave had gone.

Tintagel Cove is no sunbathing beach. The rocks and pebbles are not as inviting as nearby Trebarwith Strand or Bossiney with their expanses of soft sand. Here the atmosphere is full of mystery, charged with memories of an ancient past: It is a place to experience the wildness of the Cornish coastline, imagine the legendary figure of King Arthur, or sympathise with those early settlers who lived on the exposed headland hundreds of years before.

33595^ Tintagel, King Arthur's Castle.

# Tintagel Castle

KING Arthur's Castle stands on what has become almost an island, only connected by a narrow neck of rock which is continually under attack from the wild Atlantic Ocean. A steep track, a bridge and over one hundred steps make the castle appear inhospitable but it is well worth the effort. To enjoy a visit to Tintagel Castle you must allow plenty of time. Too many visitors arrive in the village on a tight schedule and when they discover the castle is not the magnificent building which has caught their eye on the approach to Tintagel but merely a 'pile of stones' away on an island they are disappointed and go away without ever having set foot on the Castle Track.

That enormous building which is so eye-catching from all routes into Tintagel is in fact the Castle Hotel, standing proud on the headland. It is visible in this lovely old postcard of a view of Tintagel looking back from the island but it appears as a rather vague shape. It is not steeped in history as is the castle but it has a character all of its own. Tintagel Castle has been the location for many television dramas and even the setting for a 1979 film version of *Dracula*, a very appropriate site with the towering cliffs and the ruins forming an eerie silhouette against an often fiery sky.

Many famous names have graced the splendid rooms of the Castle Hotel: Robert Taylor, Ava Gardner, Stanley Baker, Noel Coward and Donald Pleasance all stayed here whilst filming in the area. The most famous film star and actor of them all however did not. Laurence Olivier, who played Doctor Van Hesling in *Dracula,* chose to stay alone in a smaller hotel!

This second postcard looking back from the Castle Island gives a wonderful view of the castle remains on the mainland. The message on the back of the card has a familiar ring to it. Dated June 1907, the height of the summer it reads ... 'weather still very rough and stormy but managed to enjoy ourselves in spite of the rain and wind. Planned an excursion to moors and tors but alas too wet!' The summers were not always long and hot all those years ago.

This picture has been touched up by a skilful hand as there is no sigh of the village on the skyline, though it would have been visible even in 1907.

Until recently it was assumed that remains other than those of the castle itself were from an early Christian monastery of a period sometime between the fifth and ninth centuries AD. But with the more recent finds, especially those made after the fire on the island in the scorching summer of 1983, experts now are in doubt as to the nature of the occupation

19

of the island between the Roman and the Norman period. One theory is that it may have been a royal seat or at least the stronghold of some of the ruins on the top of the island though probably later than first thought. The remains of a chapel dedicated to the Celtic Saint Juliot are believed to date back to the tenth century, it has been added to at a later date, chiefly when the castle was built in the twelfth century. The castle ruins have a question mark hanging over them too. Who was responsible for the building of these fortifications and why here?

In about 1145 Earl Reginald, illegitimate son of King Henry 1, began work on a castle on the headland at Tintagel. It was to replace the makeshift Norman earthwork castle at Bossiney which lies beneath the mound there. He built the great hall, much of these walls are still visible today – an awe-inspiring sight perched high on the cliff edge, the subject of so many postcards and paintings, ancient and modern.

These old pictures show the shabby state of the ruins in the early 1900s, the grass long and unkept, no clear pathways. Compare these with recent photographs and you can clearly see the difference English Heritage makes, neat paths, mown grass and each point of interest clearly marked. The value of such sites is now more appreciated and the importance of preserving our ancient inheritance for our children is uppermost in our minds. There was never any shortage of visitors to the castle, Turner, that great English painter, Charles Dickens, Tennyson, Thackeray and many other distinguished people came here to stroll through the ruins and draw on the unique atmosphere for inspiration.

After Reginald died in 1175 the title of Earl of Cornwall was reserved for Henry II's son John. On his accession to the throne the position went to Henry Fitzcount who leased the manor of Bossiney and the castle to the de Hornacote family. They must have lived in Earl Reginald's great hall for some forty years. When King John died in 1216 his son Henry succeeded him and the lands of Cornwall were once again resumed by the crown. In 1227 the King's brother Richard was given the title Earl of Cornwall. He was an ambitious man and set about enlarging the castle at Tintagel, most of the structure visible today dates from then. Richard never actually lived at Tintagel, his main place of residence in Cornwall was at Launceston but he made his mark on Tintagel parish in other ways.

He created the Borough of Bossiney giving the inhabitants certain freedom and privileges. The boundaries can still be seen as somewhat

*These old postcards depict the romantic, if neglected, state of the Castle ruins in the early years of this century.*

*Above, a postcard sent from Tintagel in 1929 and below, a view around the same time*

larger hedges than usual, stretching from the Glebe cliffs in the south to Rocky Valley skirting behind Bossiney Mound in the north. Richard died in 1272 and from the 14th century the castle sadly slipped into decline. The Great Hall had its roof timbers removed and put into storage in the hope that better times might come. These times did come briefly when the Black Prince tried to restore the castle to its former glory. The cost of repairs however became so great that gradually the decline set in again. The Black Prince never really achieved anything for the good of the castle and as far as records can tell he never even stayed there.

By the 1500s the castle was all but a ruin, the gap between the island and the mainland had widened and interest in it had gradually diminished.

A glimmer of hope appeared in 1851 with the arrival of a new vicar in Tintagel, the Reverend Richard Bryn Kinsman. He was vicar for 43 years and in that time was responsible for the shaping of a new path to the island and generating interest in preserving the ruins. He reinstated the ancient office of 'Constable of the Castle' and wore a scarlet and gold uniform 'when conducting visitors thither'.

Tintagel Castle has had a varied past from splendour to ruin and is now carefully preserved for the future generations to walk amongst the remains laid out by their ancestors, to feel how they must have felt living on this exposed wind-swept headland. It is a place where legend mingles with truth creating a shroud of mystery. There is still so much unknown about the castle's past, so much to uncover hidden in the soil. The archaeologists of tomorrow have some surprises in store.

*The isolated and beautiful church of Tintagel.*

# Tintagel Church

THE PARISH church at Tintagel is dedicated to a mysterious, probably Welsh, saint who may have landed at Boscastle with a group of followers and settled in the area. The church at Minster, Boscastle is also believed to be dedicated to St Materiana.

In Tintagel the church enjoys a commanding position on the cliffs close by the site of Tintagel Castle. It has magnificent views and is highly visible from afar. But one might wonder why is it so isolated, so far from the village community it serves? Perhaps a preaching cross was set up here on the cliffs which may have led to the building of a small crude church. Evidence of very early graves has been found in the churchyard, small mounds which are not prehistoric or medieval but perhaps some ancient Christian burial sites. The church was reconstructed by Earl Robert at around the time of the Domesday Survey, in Norman times. It is a plain, simple shape but very impressive, inside there are few embellishments, the most outstanding feature being the huge Norman font. Work may well have already been under way before Earl Robert arrived as part of the church has a much older style showing signs of Saxon workmanship.

The churchyard contains many aspects which catch the imagination. Besides all the recent archaeological interest there are several more personal stories which touch the heart. In the very old postcard of St Materiana's there are one or two things missing from the graveyard which you would see today if you walked through it on your way to the church door. The stile remains unchanged, a beautiful piece of rustic construction. There is a similar one at the gate nearer the doorway. The long sweeping path takes you on a journey back through Tintagel's history, the names representative of the old village community.

There are some interesting epitaphs to be found. One such is written on a fine gravestone just near the church door, it is gradually becoming illegible but, you can just make out how the poor unfortunate man buried there was struck by lightning! To the right of the gate shown in the picture now stands a wooden cross mounted with a ship's lifebelt. This rather poignant symbol is a reminder of the shipwreck which occurred on December 20 1893. The *Iota* was a wooden barque built in 1866 in Bideford, after several different owners she was finally bought by a firm in Naples. She was en route from Cardiff to Trinidad laden with coal

*An old postcard shows the path leading to the church.*

when at about 5pm, in a raging sea, she was driven on to Lye Rock just off Willapark. On board was a crew of eleven men and one boy, all Italian. In desperation they tried to jump from the mast to the rock to reach safety, the onlookers who gathered on the headland could only stand and watch as the men were tossed about by the crashing sea.

Three Tintagel men showed great courage in the face of such danger; they volunteered to attempt a rescue of the men who had managed to reach the rock. It was clear that they would not survive the terrifying sea if help did not reach them quickly. One seaman and a young boy had already tried to swim ashore but had perished. The Tintagel men led by Thomas Brown knew they had to act swiftly. The other men with Brown were Charles Hambly and the blacksmith Glanville. They were joined by a coastguard by the name of Hughes. It was pitch dark by the time the tide allowed these brave men to climb onto the Rock but with the sea still raging and though unable to speak a word of Italian, they managed to reassure the crew that help was at hand.

Charles Hambly displayed enormous courage by working his way down to the men using a rope, and one by one they were all brought up

Stone cross in
Tintagel Churchyard

*The simple stone cross in the churchyard – a drawing by Felicity Young.*

27

Tintagel Church

and swung across to the mainland by coastguard's cradle. In all nine of the crew were rescued but the body of the 14-year-old boy was washed ashore and a sad procession carried it through Bossiney into the village. The boy, Domenico Catanese, was buried at Tintagel, his service conducted partly in Latin for the benefit of his fellow countrymen. His grave is marked by an oak cross and a lifebelt from the wrecked ship. It remains a symbol of the great heroism and of the terrible tragedy of that December night. Charles Hambly later received an award for his bravery from the King of Italy.

The other important feature missing from the postcard is the war memorial which is obviously a more 'modern' addition to the churchyard. It lists the men of Tintagel who lost their lives during the war and like all memorials throughout the country is decked with poppies on Remembrance Day. The weather is not always very respectful and often the wreaths are battered by the strong winds which ravage the headland in winter: a sad reminder of our vulnerability.

*A place to contemplate.*

# Trebarwith

NOT FAR from Tintagel, heading in a southerly direction you will find a narrow valley winding down to the sea. At first sight it does not look very promising, a huge rock strangely called Gull Rock in the shape of a dog's head fills your view and it makes you wonder just what lies ahead; but as you approach the little cluster of buildings the surf can be seen pounding on the sand in the distance. The beach is approached by a narrow gully which cuts its way through the rock opening out onto a magnificent expanse of fine sand.

Here is one of Cornwall's finest surfing beaches. Much of the building which has taken place at Trebarwith is linked to the tourism which inevitably grew up in such a beautiful spot. The Strand Hotel occupies a prominent position along the road and in recent years there have sprung up icecream kiosks and 'surf' shops. High up on the cliff overlooking the mile-long strand is what is now a public house; on a warm summer evening there is no better place to watch a glorious Cornish sunset than from the front of the Port William. The inn gets its name from the little cove just around the point to the left of Trebarwith Strand, once the scene of a certain amount of seaborne trade.

The actual village of Trebarwith is some little way away from the hubbub of the beach and its trappings of surfers in brightly coloured wetsuits, carrying boards under their arms, and sunbathers wearing hats and sandals and little else. Having tackled the steep hill known as Black Hill to the south you enter a different world. The tiny hamlet was part of the manor of Trebarwith, there are not many houses and there is a wonderful feeling of tranquility, the huge farmhouse being the focal point. There is a footpath which starts here and takes you down to the cove known as 'Backways'. It is well worth the hike through a beautiful valley over rugged terrain, a little known part of North Cornwall.

Trebarwith Strand.

"STRAND RESIDENTIAL HOTEL", TINTAGEL.

332  Trebarwith Valley

# Prince of Wales Quarry & Engine House

QUARRYING for slate has been an important industry in Cornwall since the 1400s. It is widely used in building the renowned Cornish stone walls and for roofing slates. The largest and perhaps the best known quarry in North Cornwall is Delabole but the parish of Tintagel has many smaller ones, some still in operation today. Extensive quarrying took place around Trebarwith where Penpethy, Jeffray's Pit, Bolehill and the Prince of Wales quarries were once worked. At high tide the slate was loaded onto boats for export from Trebarwith Strand. Donkeys were used to carry the slate down from the quarries, negotiating a rough track to the sea. Today the roads are reasonably wide and access to the beach from higher up the valley is easy: hard to imagine what it must have been like in the days of limited transport and no labour saving machinery.

One of the most spectacular quarries in this area is the Prince of Wales quarry. It was working during the mid 19th century, occupying a site in the valley near Trewarmett. From the top of the quarry there are splendid views of the coast, Gull Rock at Trebarwith stands out clearly, the focal point in the panorama.

A waterfall cascades into a lake formed in the 'hole' created by the workings of the quarrymen. The trees are sparse and wind-swept, the bracken and brambles have crept in to give the place an intentional air of dereliction. The site is owned by the Duchy of Cornwall and leased to North Cornwall District Council which has undertaken to protect the wonderful variety of wildlife which has taken over the site. There is a wealth of typically Cornish wild flowers, birds, butterflies and even dragonflies to be seen while clambering up the slate-clad slopes towards the engine-house which stands like a sentinel above the now tranquil quarry. The engine-house was carefully restored by the Prince of Wales Engine House Society in 1976, a monument to our Cornish heritage.

But the building is no longer alive with the sound of the huge beam engine, the slate steps leading up to the engine house no longer echo with the sound of workers' feet upon them as they trudge to work at dawn each day, nor does the valley ring with the sound of tools on stone. A lone buzzard or a few jackdaws provide the only company as you stand before the open doorway of the engine-house. It evokes a kind of sadness: the passing of an era.

Engine House, Prince of Wales Quarry, Tintagel.

35

Felicity May '83

The Old Post Office, Tintagel.

# Willapark

THERE are few more breathtaking places to rest on your walk between Tintagel and Boscastle than here on the headland at Willapark. A well positioned bench makes the stopping even better as it faces towards Lundy Island and the coast of North Devon. You can see the white dishes of the radio tracking station at Morwenstow quite clearly on certain days, this goes for Lundy as well. There is a saying that if you can see Lundy then it is about to rain and if you can't see Lundy it is raining already! This somewhat insults the Cornish climate as the weather can be extremely good as well as bad. I am sure that is the same anywhere but we do have some terrific storms being so exposed to the full force of the Atlantic Ocean. Gale force winds tend to make walking on these headlands somewhat dangerous, so it is no wonder that people are inclined to 'hibernate' here in winter months. Only a few brave souls take to the footpaths to walk the dog and breathe in the invigorating sea air.

In the summer months bird watchers have been known to gather at Willapark in the hope of glimpsing a puffin. There is a fine collection of sea birds inhabiting these cliffs. If you are very lucky you might even see the seals which sometimes play in the waters off Bossiney and Benouth, or even a lazy basking shark sloping through the crystal clear water beneath the cliffs. The spring and summer sees a most wonderful array of wild flowers, bringing the headlands alive with colour and buzzing with insects.

If I make this part of the coast sound like a paradise it is because I feel it is very *special*, I spend a lot of time walking this stretch of the coastal footpath and the piece either side of Tintagel has, I believe, a unique atmosphere.

*Two views of the headland – one captured on film by Ray Bishop, the sun casting interesting shadows around the rocks and adding a shimmer to the calm sea and, opposite, a pen and ink sketch by Felicity Young, conveying the essence of this atmospheric part of the coast.*

As an artist I am very aware of the strong shapes of the rocks, creating the powerful relationship between the ever moving sea and solid unchanging land. Then there are the vivid colours, especially in spring and summer when the clifftops are strewn with wild flowers and the narrow lanes with their high hedges and typically Cornish walls and banks are a multitude of shade: pink, blue, green and yellow. In winter the sea can produce some powerful colours, deep blues and greens, so clear that you can see the bottom. But only the very brave and properly dressed would dare enter these icy waters. The strong winds that blow south-westerly in the winter can quickly whip the sea into a frenzy, an awe-inspiring sight … making a mere mortal feel very vulnerable even at a distance on the clifftop.

41

# Bossiney Cove

BOSSINEY Cove provides us with yet another secluded beach, again not the easiest of approaches, down steep, often slippery steps cut into the rock but this makes it all the more attractive as it is not overcrowded in summer. Here too is an atmosphere all its own. Some days the sun is slow to reach the tiny beach and there is a shiver in the air. The cliffs on either side tower above, almost as though they want to crowd in on top of you.

One very curious feature of the cove, which is best viewed from above on the way down to the beach, is the strange rock formation known as Elephant Rock, an odd natural phenomenon where the erosion by the sea has caused a fault, forming an arch. The impression created is that of a majestic elephant standing at the entrance to some mighty palace.

It is hard to imagine a string of donkeys trailing up from such an inaccessible beach but these surefooted creatures toiled up and down the rocky path, making three trips a day carrying sand for a retired fisherman in the late eighteen hundreds.

Bossiney then a cove and beach of considerable character – and individuality – and this is symbolic. Sonia and Michael Williams, when they came to Bossiney in 1965, recall that many local people insisted their addresses read 'Bossiney, Tintagel'. Bossiney residents firmly maintained 'We are not Tintagel.'

There is though something of a paradox. That Elephant Rock, which I have drawn for an earlier Bossiney title, brings an international air to this very Cornish cove – and that too is symbolic.

Times were when Cornwall sent miners abroad. Cornish ships sailed the seas and traded with other countries. Cornishmen served in the Royal Navy and the Merchant Navy and, of course, Cornwall's own regiment was based not many miles away at Bodmin.

So Elephant Rock, in a curious way, reflects something of Cornwall and Cornish people – a willingness to look out and away from home when necessary.

*Looking north from Bossiney Lands. The coastline here at Tintagel must be some of the most spectacular anywhere in Cornwall. To live in such a place is a privilege. I frequently walk along these cliffs to remind myself just how lucky I am to have this kind of wild, unspoilt scenery almost in my back garden.*

*An interesting fact about this picture is that Ray Bishop took it in mid-winter – a reminder that we have some good days outside the holiday season. Over the years Ray has taken dozens of photographs of this part of the coastline.*

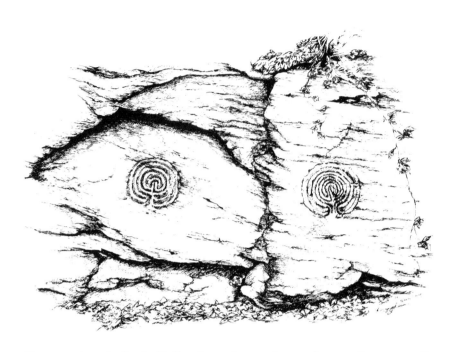

*Rare carvings in Rocky Valley. Legacies, perhaps, of some distant or religious rite.*

Michael Williams recalls doing his first piece of television film in and around Rocky Valley and Bossiney in the 1960s. 'I felt very nervous and aware of the cameras. Only later did I learn from Clive Gunnell, that wise television walker, the trick of simply talking to the interviewer and ignoring everything else. Clive's television walks are still going strong and I have never forgotten his advice.'

In view of the scenery and the legends, it is only natural that television and film companies have been drawn to this area. The visual qualities are full of power and variety.

# Rocky Valley

NOW we come to the last destination on our Tintagel tour.

Canyon-like and somehow Gothic, Rocky Valley looks and feels like a location that might have come straight out of a novel by Dame Iris Murdoch.

We have known people who have come here once and never returned. We have known others who find it an energising experience and keep returning. There is *something* here.

In this valley lies a brace of ancient secrets. Shaped into the Boscastle side amid ruins are two rare Labyrinth Pattern Carvings, dating from the Early Bronze Age, 1800 to 1400 BC. Ancient Kernow knows nothing like them, their purpose shrouded in mystery.

We have stood in front of them and speculated about the person or persons who carved these strange patterns. Are they legacies of some old magic or religion?

At Bossiney, years ago, we heard of a psychic investigator who wanted to find out the truth. He persuaded a young woman to undergo hypnosis at the very spot. She regressed, went back to another time and emerged from her regression in a very distressed condition, believing some form of human sacrifice had taken place.,

The puzzle deepens in that the maze patterns are to be found on ancient coins from Knossos, a sacred symbol among Hopi Indians and a religious emblem in India.

What inspired them? How are Tintagel and India linked? Who carved them?

Some places pose more questions than they answer. Often in seeking a solution we stumble across another query – and that maybe is why Rocky Valley remains so strange and beautiful.

## MORE BOSSINEY BOOKS …

**KING ARTHUR IN THE WEST**
by Felicity Young and Michael Williams

**NORTH CORNWALL REFLECTIONS**
by Hilda Hambly

**BODMIN MOOR THROUGH THE YEARS**
by EV Thompson

**CURIOSITIES OF EXMOOR**
by Felicity Young
*'… a tour in words and pictures of the National Park embracing Somerset and Devon.'* **Nancy Hammonds, Evening Herald**
*'Felicity Young, an artist who has contributed many drawings to Bossiney Books, makes her debut as an author with a beautiful description of Exmoor and its many delights.'*
**June Glover, South Hams Group of Newspapers.**

**SECRET CORNWALL**
Introduced by Madeleine Gould

**PSYCHIC PHENOMENA OF THE WEST**
by Michael Williams

**GHOSTS & PHANTOMS OF THE WEST**
by Peter Underwood

**LEGENDS OF CORNWALL**
by Sally Jones


**STRANGE STORIES OF CORNWALL**
Six writers prove that fact is often stranger than fiction.
*'Thought-provoking ... little-known occurrences, strange places and eccentric characters'.* **Adrian Ruck, Cornish and Devon Post.**

**KING ARTHUR COUNTRY**
by Brenda Duxbury, Michael Williams and Colin Wilson
An exciting exploration of the Arthurian sites in Cornwall, includes the related legend of Tristan and Iseult.

We shall be pleased to send you our catalogue, giving full details of our growing list of titles for Cornwall, Devon, Dorset, Somerset, Avon and Wiltshire. If you have difficulty in obtaining our titles, write direct to Bossiney Books, Land's End, St Teath, Bodmin, Cornwall.